HOW? WHO? WHAT? WHEN? WHERE? WHY?

Questions Kids ask

ABOUT
FAMOUS PEOPLE

GROLIER
BOOKS

CONTRIBUTORS

Alison Dickie	Pamela Martin	Jocelyn Smyth
Bill Ivy	Colin McCance	Merebeth Switzer
Jacqueline Kendel	Nancy Prasad	Dave Taylor
Ann Langdon	Robin Rivers	Alison Tharen
Sheila Macdonald	Lois Rock	Donna Thomson
Susan Marshall		Pam Young

INTERIOR ART AND DESIGN

Richard Comely	Greg Elliott	Richard Migliore
George Elliott	Ernie Homewood	Sue Wilkinson

First published in Canada
by Grolier Limited 1989
16 Overlea Blvd., Toronto, Ontario M5H 1A6
Telephone (416) 425-1924; Fax (416) 425-8858

Canadian Cataloguing in Publication Data

Questions kids ask about famous people

(Questions kids ask ; 6)
ISBN 0-7172-2545-3 (bound) — ISBN 0-7172-2823-1 (pbk)

1. Biography—Miscellanea—Juvenile literature.
2. Celebrities—Miscellanea—Juvenile literature.
3. Children's questions and answers.
I. Smyth, Jocelyn. II. Comely, Richard. III. Series.

CT107.Q47   1988   j920'.02   C89-093159-3

Paperback:
Cover design: Tania Craan
Cover art: Amanda Duffy

Casebound:
Cover design: Richard Comely
Cover art: Richard Comely

Questions Kids Ask . . . about FAMOUS PEOPLE

continued

Who was King Tut?

One of the most exciting archaeological discoveries ever was made in Egypt in 1922. An archaeologist (a person who studies past civilizations) named Howard Carter was searching an area known as the Valley of the Kings when he came upon a tomb no one knew about.

Since all the other tombs in the valley had been robbed long before by grave diggers, Carter was fearful that this one too had been damaged. When he and his crew excavated the tomb, they found that grave robbers had indeed entered it, but they had been foiled by hidden traps.

In the inner chambers of the tomb, Carter discovered one of the finest arrays of early Egyptian artifacts ever found. These included a solid gold coffin, a gold mask and many precious jewels and gold carvings. These incredible riches had been buried with a young king known as Tutankhamen, who ruled Egypt from 1361 to 1352 B.C. He became pharaoh at age 9 and died at age 18.

DID YOU KNOW . . . a curse was supposedly placed on all who broke into King Tut's tomb, and in fact Carter and many of his party did die under unusual circumstances.

Who invented the printing press?

Before 1455 books took a long time to make since they had to be copied out by hand. This meant that books were expensive and not widely available, especially to people who were not wealthy. This changed when Johann Gutenberg, a German goldsmith, invented a printing press using movable type.

Gutenberg started printing with carved wooden blocks, a method used for hundreds of years in the Orient. These blocks were similar to the rubber stamps with raised letters that we use today. But Gutenberg carved raised letters, or type, for a whole page of a book on one piece of wood. The problem with this method was that the letters on the block could not be rearranged to form new words.

Gutenberg decided to make individual letters out of brass. Then he set them on a flat surface. Using a special ink created for use on metals he printed the type on paper using a press much like a wine press which crushes grapes. The result after more experiments was the Gutenberg Bible, the first printed book in Europe.

Who was Shakespeare?

William Shakespeare was the greatest poet and playwright of the English-speaking world. Over 370 years after his death, his plays are being performed more often and in more places than ever before.

Little is known about Shakespeare's early life, other than that he was born in 1564 in Stratford on the river Avon in England. At age 18 he married a woman named Anne Hathaway with whom he had three children.

By 1592 Shakespeare was working as an actor in London. Times were difficult because a plague had hit the city and the theaters were forced to close. He had to rely on his skills as a writer to make a living.

When the theaters reopened in 1594, Shakespeare and some actor friends began their own acting company. It became a great success and they were soon able to build their own theater.

Shakespeare wrote many of his best works for the company and even acted in them on stage. His plots were often based on the lives of historical figures, such as Julius Caesar and Henry IV. Perhaps his best known work is *Romeo and Juliet,* a sad story about two young people in love who came from families that hated each other. He also wrote two long narrative poems and 154 sonnets.

Unbelievable as it may seem, Shakespeare's plays existed only as working scripts throughout his lifetime. After his death in 1616, two of his friends collected 36 of his plays and had them published. If not for them, the plays might have been lost forever.

How many wives did Henry VIII have?

Henry VIII was king of England in the 16th century. He is as famous for the number of his wives as for anything else he did as king. Henry married six times, divorcing or beheading a wife each time he grew bored with her or impatient because she didn't bear a son to succeed him as king.

Being the wife of Henry VIII was thus very chancy. He annuled, or canceled, his marriage to his first wife. He chopped off the head of his second wife, Anne Boleyn, following the birth of a daughter. Henry's third wife died shortly after giving birth to a son who died at age 15. He divorced his fourth wife. His fifth wife suffered the same fate as her cousin, Henry's second wife. She, too, lost her head to the executioner's blade. Henry's sixth and last wife, Catherine Parr, was lucky. Henry died before he could dispose of her. She died a peaceful death one year later.

Who was Bonnie Prince Charlie?

Bonnie Prince Charlie's real name was Charles Edward Stuart, and he was a descendant of a long line of Scottish and English monarchs. The British crown had passed into the hands of the Hanovers, and Charles wanted to restore his family as rulers of Britain.

With only his dash and charm, Bonnie Prince Charlie convinced Scottish clansmen to join him in his battle. They left Scotland and won several victories over the Hanoverian forces, but they were eventually defeated. With the help of loyal supporters, Charlie escaped capture and fled to France. He was later expelled from France and settled in Italy. Many romantic stories and ballads were written about him and his bold attempt to capture the crown.

Who was Sitting Bull?

Sitting Bull was a great chief of the Sioux Indians of the American Northwest. He was brave, generous, wise and legendary as a medicine man and warrior. Along with Crazy Horse, another Sioux chief, Sitting Bull led the last major Indian resistance against the United States government's efforts to move the Sioux off their traditional lands and onto reservations. At the Battle of Little Bighorn in 1876, they rallied a vast force of Sioux and Cheyenne and won a stunning victory over United States cavalry troops led by General George Custer. Defeat only strengthened the government's resolve, however, and within a few months, the Sioux were forced out of the area by white settlers. Sitting Bull fled to Canada with 3000 members of his tribe. They were forced to go back by the Canadian government, which was afraid of problems similar to those in the United States. Sitting Bull spent two years in prison, then settled on a Dakota reservation. He was killed by police in 1890 during another protest against the United States government.

DID YOU KNOW . . . Sitting Bull was a member of Buffalo Bill's Wild West Show for a year or two.

Who was Buffalo Bill?

Buffalo Bill was an American frontiersman whose real name was William Frederick Cody. He got his nickname because he was an expert marksman and supplied large quantities of buffalo meat to workers building a railroad in Kansas. Buffalo Bill rode a mule in a messenger service, made trips west with wagon trains and rode on a mail route for the famous pony express. He was active during the Civil War with an anti-slavery organization called Jayhawk.

Between 1868 and 1872 he worked as an army scout and served as a guide for buffalo hunters. Although he won the Congressional Medal of Honor for gallantry in 1872, Congress revoked the medal because he wasn't a member of the military at the time.

In 1883 Buffalo Bill started his famous Wild West show, which featured roundups, mock stage robberies and buffalo hunts. The performers included Annie Oakley, ''Wild Bill'' Hickok and ''Texas Jack'' Omohundro. One of the highlights of this show was a mock battle with Indians during which Buffalo Bill demonstrated his amazing shooting ability. He toured with the show throughout Europe and the United States for 20 years.

Buffalo Bill died in 1917. His grave is located on Lookout Mountain near the town of Golden, Colorado.

11

Who was the Red Baron?

In the First World War, the Germans painted their fighter aircraft in brilliant colors and garish designs, so the British and Canadian pilots called the German squadrons "flying circuses." The Richthofen Circus commanded by the deadly Red Baron was the most feared of all the flying circuses.

The Red Baron was Baron Manfred von Richthofen, who flew a bright red Fokker triplane (a triplane has three wings, one above the other). Richthofen was the top air ace of the war. He shot down a total of 80 aircraft piloted by English, Canadian, Australian and French airmen.

One day in April 1918, a group of Allied fighters dove into the Richthofen Circus. Each man lost track of everything except the airplane in front of him, as the fighters maneuvered to shoot at each other and to avoid being shot. When the two sides finally separated, the Red Baron had gone down. His red triplane was found behind the Allied lines, with the Red Baron sitting dead in the cockpit, a bullet through his heart.

Who was Amelia Earhart?

Born in Kansas in 1898, Amelia Earhart was one of the world's aviation pioneers. She was the first woman passenger on a transatlantic flight, and in 1932 she became the first woman pilot to make a solo flight across the north Atlantic.

Three years later, Amelia Earhart became the first pilot ever to fly across the Pacific Ocean. This journey took her from Hawaii's Oahu Island to the United States mainland in

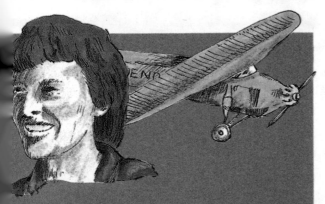

California. This trip lasted 18 hours and 15 minutes.

Sadly, in July of 1937, Amelia Earhart and her navigator were lost over the Pacific Ocean between New Guinea and Howland Island while attempting to fly around the world.

Who was the Lone Eagle?

Charles Lindbergh, one of the most famous pilots who ever lived, was nicknamed ''the Lone Eagle'' after his famous flight from New York to Paris in 1927. This flight made him the first person to fly alone across the Atlantic Ocean.

Lindberg made the trip in a plane he called *The Spirit of St. Louis.* It had only one engine and just enough room for Lindbergh to sit in it. He left New York in the early morning of May 20, 1927 and landed near Paris 33 hours and 30 minutes later. He had flown over 5800 kilometres (3600 miles). More than 100 000 cheering people were waiting for him at the Paris airfield, and he immediately became an international hero. He received medals for his courage and skill from countries all over the world.

Lindbergh's flight was important not only because he was the first person to make the trip, but also because the flight helped people to understand the usefulness of the airplane.

Which king of Israel was famous for his wisdom?

Solomon was the king of Israel from 972 to 922 B.C. His rule was a time of peace for the country. Relying more upon his intelligence than his sword, he kept Israel safe and helped it to prosper. He built a huge temple in Jerusalem, a royal palace and a fleet of ships. He soon became famous throughout many lands for his great wealth and wisdom.

A well-known story tells how Solomon settled an argument between two women. Each claimed to be the mother of a small baby. Since no one could tell who was speaking the truth, Solomon devised a clever plan. He ordered a sword to be brought and proposed to cut the child into two equal parts. Each woman, he declared, would receive one of the halves. One woman agreed to the decision, but the other immediately gave up her claim, begging Solomon to spare the child's life. The king had found the true mother. He knew that the real parent would rather give up the baby than see it harmed.

Not everyone was happy with Solomon's rule. Many citizens were angered by his high-handed ways and the heavy taxes he made them pay. Nonetheless, it is mainly for his wisdom that he is remembered today.

Who was Confucius?

Confucius was a Chinese philosopher who lived almost 2500 years ago. His teachings are called Confucianism. Confucianism is not a religion, but a philosophy which tells people how to live a wise and good life.

Confucius taught a way of "right living." His philosophy instructs people to treat others as

Who was Catherine the Great?

Catherine II, Empress of Russia, left her mark on history by helping to transform Russia into a modern country. She came to power when army officers led a coup against her husband, the unpopular Peter III.

Catherine planned many reforms to help the common people. She encouraged the modernization of agriculture and industry, promoted learning and improved schools and universities. Later, however, she abandoned these ideas and returned the privileges of the ruling class.

Under Catherine's rule, Russian generals won much territory in Poland and the Crimea. St. Petersburg (now Leningrad) began to rival Paris as a cultural center as the Empress brought to her court many of the talented artists of the period. Catherine supported Italian opera, painting, sculpture and architecture and popularized French literature and liberal philosophy.

Catherine the Great transformed Russia into one of Europe's most powerful and influential states.

they themselves would like to be treated, whether they are rich or poor, kings or servants. It also teaches people to behave properly in their friendships and relationships with everyone they meet. The beliefs of Confucius, therefore, can be applied to all areas of life. Many people still follow the philosophy today.

Who was Genghis Khan?

Between Russia and China lies Mongolia, a harsh, mountainous land with extreme temperatures and very little water. From this place about 800 years ago, a group of warriors rode out to create one of the greatest empires the world has ever known. They were the Mongols.

In 1167 a boy was born to one of the Mongol tribes. His name was Temujin, and he grew to be a fierce warrior. Using a combination of discipline, cunning and ruthlessness, he gathered an army of loyal supporters. By 1206 Temujin had conquered all the Mongol clans. He took the title *Genghis Khan* which means "universal ruler."

Genghis Khan was not satisfied with just being the ruler of the Mongols. His armies soon began to conquer northern China, Russia and Central Asia. Wherever they went they spread terror among the people.

When Genghis Khan died in 1227, the empire stretched from the Black Sea in the west to the Pacific Ocean in the east.

DID YOU KNOW . . . the Mongols used arrows that could pierce armor and were capable of killing at distances of over 180 metres (600 feet)!

16

Who crossed the Alps with elephants?

Hannibal was a brilliant general who lived more than 2000 years ago. His father was a leader of the Carthaginians. Carthage was a powerful city-state in north Africa and it wanted to control southern Europe. The rival of Carthage was the Roman Empire.

At the age of 10 Hannibal swore eternal hatred to Rome. At 26 he became commander of the Carthaginian army in Spain. When he captured the Spanish city of Saguntum, the Romans declared war on him. Hannibal decided to surprise them by invading northern Italy. He set out with 40 000 soldiers and 38 elephants to cross the Pyrenees Mountains, southern France and the Alps into Italy. It was winter, and Hannibal lost most of his elephants and many soldiers along the way, but he astonished the Roman forces and won many battles.

While he was in Italy, the Romans attacked Carthage itself. Hannibal was called to the city's defense but was defeated. He fled and joined Syrian troops against the Romans but they too lost. Refusing to be taken prisoner by the Romans, Hannibal poisoned himself.

Who was Einstein?

Albert Einstein is generally considered to have been the greatest genius of the 20th century. Although he developed a whole new way of looking at the nature of the universe, his name is forever linked to the atomic age because his theories led to the development of the atomic bomb. This horrified him since he was devoted to the cause of peace.

Albert Einstein was born in southern Germany in 1879. There is a well-known story that he failed mathematics in school, but it isn't true. He was, however, expelled from high school for having a bad attitude. Eventually, he got a university degree and went to work in a patent office in Switzerland. Soon afterwards he began his great discoveries.

His theory of relativity made him famous. This theory contained a number of revolutionary ideas about the nature of physical reality, expressed in the language of mathematics. Although few people understood it and it took years to prove it, people recognized that Einstein was a genius. He was invited to lecture at universities all over the world. In 1933 he moved to the United States and worked at a university where he could do research at his own pace. Until his death in 1955 he continued to search for laws to explain the universe.

Who was Helen Keller?

Helen Keller was 19 months old when an illness made her blind and deaf, and as a result of the deafness, mute (unable to speak). For years she could only communicate through laughter and tantrums.

Then, with the help of a dedicated teacher, Anne Sullivan, Keller learned a special type of sign language. They used touch on the hands to convey words and ideas. She later learned how to read braille, to write using a special typewriter and even to speak.

Helen Keller went on to earn a university degree in 1904 and to lecture in many countries to raise money for the education of handicapped people.

Who was Martin Luther King Jr.?

Martin Luther King Jr. was the leader of the non-violent movement for the rights of the poor, disadvantaged and racially oppressed in the United States. His campaigns for equality started in 1955 when he led a year-long boycott of buses in Alabama and continued across the country. Eventually they led the Supreme Court to rule that segregation (separation) of whites and blacks in public places was against the law. King's actions helped bring about the 1964 Civil Rights Act and the 1965 Voting Rights Act which guaranteed equality for blacks.

For his civil rights work, Martin Luther King Jr. received the Nobel Peace Prize in 1964. He was assassinated in 1968, but his work lives on and his birth date, January 15, is now a national holiday in the United States.

Who was Joan of Arc?

Joan of Arc was born in 1412 on a farm in France. When she was 13, she began to hear voices and see visions of saints and the archangel Michael. The voices told her that she must bring peace to her country. France and England were fighting what is now called the Hundred Years' War.

France was controlled by a group of nobles from the province of Burgundy. The Burgundians had joined with the English and taken control of the country when the king, Charles VI, died in 1422. The king's son, Dauphin Charles, had gone into hiding, and Joan thought that the best way to end the war with England was to make it possible for Charles to become King of France.

Joan met with Charles, and he agreed to let her lead his soldiers to the city of Orleans, which the English were trying to capture. Joan was only 17 when she led the troops into battle. She fought with courage and skill and won her first great victory.

Joan won more battles and proved that she was a genius at leading soldiers. Under her leadership, the French soldiers won back enough land for Charles to be crowned King of France.

The English and their Burgundian allies still controlled parts of France, however, so Joan continued to fight. Her last battle was an attack on Paris. When her troops lost, Joan was captured by the Burgundians and sold to the English.

DID YOU KNOW . . . once Charles VII was crowned, Joan stopped hearing voices and seeing visions.

The English claimed that Joan's visions had come from the devil and charged her with witchcraft. She was sentenced to death. On May 30, 1431, at the age of 19, Joan of Arc was burned at the stake. But people did not forget her great courage. In 1920 the Roman Catholic Church declared Joan a saint and she is still a beloved French national heroine.

What was Michelangelo famous for?

Born in Florence in 1475, Michelangelo Buonarroti excelled in painting, sculpture and architecture and was one of the most important artists of the Renaissance. His statue of David is probably his most famous. It stands 4.3 metres (14 feet) high and was carved from a single block of marble that other sculptors felt was unworkable.

In 1508, the artist was asked to decorate the ceiling of the Vatican's Sistine Chapel with scenes from the Old Testament of the Bible. This commission took four years to complete and included 343 figures. The work was particularly difficult since the artist had to lie on his back on scaffolding to paint. Michelangelo later produced magnificent wall paintings for the altar of the Sistine chapel.

He was the architect of St. Peter's Basilica. From 1547 until his death in 1564, he undertook the design and building of the Basilica's great dome. This and his other designs influenced the architecture of many countries.

Who was Walt Disney?

You've probably heard of Disneyland and Disneyworld, and you've certainly heard of Donald Duck and Mickey Mouse. Well, Walt Disney designed these remarkable theme parks and he is the creator of Donald and Mickey.

Born in 1901, Walt Disney grew up on a farm in Missouri, then studied art in Chicago. In 1923 he moved to Los Angeles to try his hand at making animated films. The going was tough at first, and he barely made a living from the cartoons he drew in a make-shift studio in a garage.

Everything changed when the first Mickey Mouse cartoons were released in 1928 with Disney himself providing the voice for Mickey. They were an instant hit and from then on Disney moved from one success to another. He made the first technicolor film in 1932, and his first full-length movie, *Snow White and the Seven Dwarfs,* is one of the most popular films ever made. His other famous animated films include *Pinocchio, Fantasia, Dumbo, Bambi, Cinderella* and *The Jungle Book.*

Disney later moved away from animation to make films with real animals or human actors. *Mary Poppins,* which combines actors and animation, is the most successful of his later films.

23

Who was Johnny Appleseed?

For 40 years in the late 18th and early 19th century, a wandering pioneer by the name of John Chapman traveled through the Ohio River region, planting and tending apple orchards everywhere he went. Affectionately known as Johnny Appleseed, Chapman inspired many legends and became an American folk hero.

Who was Lawrence of Arabia?

Thomas Edward Lawrence first came to know the Arabs through archaeological work in the Middle East. He soon learned the Arab customs, philosophies and language.

In 1916, as a British colonel, he was sent to help free the Arabs from Turkish rule. He organized the troops in capturing key areas and, after many battles, he and the Arabs defeated the Turks and forced them out of western Arabia and Syria. In 1918 the Arabs took the city of Damascus and Lawrence returned to Britain.

Lawrence attended the Paris

Who was the lady with the lamp?

Florence Nightingale is the founder of modern nursing. During the Crimean War in the mid 1800s, Florence was asked by the British government to lead a group of nurses to the war front to care for the wounded soldiers. She quickly realized that more deaths were caused by the dirty and overcrowded conditions in the military hospitals than by wounds. Against great odds, she succeeded in improving conditions and in reducing the death rate of the wounded

soldiers from 42 percent to 2 percent.

She is known as the lady with the lamp because she worked night and day during the Crimean War and was often seen walking through the wards at night with a lit lamp. After the war she returned to England and founded a nursing school in London. Her system of nursing was soon adopted around the world.

Peace Conference of 1919 to defend Arab interests in the peace negotiations. He arrived in full Arab dress, shocking and angering representatives of some European countries. He served for a time as Middle Eastern advisor to the British government and later wrote of his Arabian adventures in *The Seven Pillars of Wisdom*.

What was Captain Cook famous for?

Born in 1728, the great British explorer Captain James Cook was famous for many reasons.

After he charted previously unknown territory along the eastern coast of Canada, the Royal Navy sent him to map the South Pacific. One of his tasks was to find *Terra australis incognita,* a southern continent that was known only in legends. He was also asked to study the passage of the planet Venus as it came between the earth and the sun.

Cook left England in the *Endeavour* in August 1768. Eight months later he arrived in Tahiti. He spent three months there so the ship's scientists could study plant and animal species on the island. Cook then sailed toward New Zealand, and in 1770 he discovered the southeast coast of Australia, which he named New South Wales.

Cook charted the coasts of New Zealand and Australia but found no trace of the mysterious southern continent. The *Endeavour* sailed back to England.

Captain Cook returned to the

- - - - 1768-71
———— 1772-75
.... 1776-79
✕ Killed

N

EUROPE

INDI

AFRICA

CAPE OF GOOD HOPE

KERGUELEN ISLANDS

South Pacific in 1772 to fill in details on earlier maps. The ship sailed to the Cape of Good Hope, off the southern coast of Africa, then became the first ship ever to cross the Antarctic Circle. In just three years Cook traveled over 113 000 kilometres (70 000 miles)!

On his third and final journey to the Pacific, Cook discovered the Hawaiian Islands and Christmas Island. Searching for a northwest passage around the top of North America, he sailed to Nootka Sound, near Vancouver.

The ship headed up the coast of what is now North America to the Arctic Ocean but did not locate the passage. Cook sailed south to Hawaii. During the winter, Polynesian natives stole one of the British ships and killed Captain Cook.

Although Cook did not find the Northwest Passage or Antarctica, he did make many valuable discoveries in exploring the South Pacific and North America.

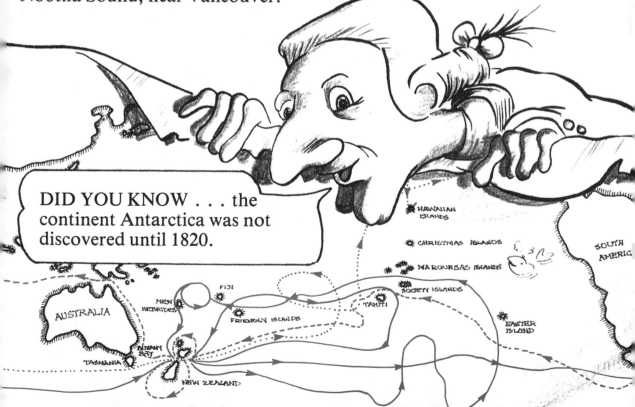

DID YOU KNOW . . . the continent Antarctica was not discovered until 1820.

Who was composing music at five years of age?

Wolfgang Amadeus Mozart was only five years old when he began composing minuets and other piano pieces. He completed his first symphony at age 9 and his first opera at 12.

His musician father began to teach Mozart and his older sister music when they were very young. By the time he was four, Mozart could memorize short pieces and play them perfectly.

DID YOU KNOW . . . Mozart was so busy composing music and touring that he never went to school.

When he was only six, Mozart went with his father and sister on a concert tour through Europe. They played for a German prince in Munich, then they performed for the empress in Vienna. They proceeded to Brussels and Paris, gave concerts at the French king's palace at Versailles, then went to London and Holland. Finally they returned to Austria.

Mozart went on to become the composer for the archbishop of Salzburg, court organist, composer for the emperor, and later a teacher in Vienna. Although he is now considered one of the world's greatest musical geniuses, he died in poverty at the age of 35. His reputation had faded as he grew older and his music was thought to be too complex and emotional by the society of the day.

Who were the Beatles?

Is there really anyone out there who doesn't recognize the name of this wildly popular group? Or who can't rattle off the names of its members: Ringo Starr, Paul McCartney, John Lennon, George Harrison?

But what if we asked you who were the Beat Boys, the Quarrymen, Johnny and the Moondogs, the Silver Beatles and The Rainbow? Answer: the Beatles before they came up with the name and the sound that clicked.

This British rock group led a musical invasion of the world between 1962 and 1970. They toured North America, Europe, the Soviet Union and the Far East, and before they disbanded in 1970, they had more number one records than any other artist or group in history—20 in all.

For ten years fans hoped for a reunion of the Beatles. Then all such hopes were dashed when John Lennon was murdered in New York in 1980. The other members still record and perform individually, and the Beatles' profound influence on popular music is still felt today.

Who was the first person to walk on the moon?

Have you ever wondered what it would be like to stand on the moon and look up at the earth?

The first person to find out was the American astronaut Neil Armstrong. On July 20, 1969, he stepped out of his spacecraft called *The Eagle,* and became the first person to walk on the moon. It certainly was a giant step. Armstrong and his partner, Edwin Aldrin Jr., explored the area around their ship, and collected rock samples and performed experiments that told us much about what it's really like on the moon.

Whose faces are carved into Mount Rushmore?

Mount Rushmore stands in the Black Hills of South Dakota. What is so special about this mountain? One of the biggest sculptures in the world is carved into one of its sides! The sculpture, started in 1927 by Gutzon Borglum, took 14 years to complete.

If you were going to carve a sculpture in a mountain what would you choose to carve? Borglum chose to carve the head and shoulders of four American presidents—George Washington, Abraham Lincoln, Thomas Jefferson and Theodore Roosevelt. The heads alone are 18 metres (60 feet) high and can be seen from almost 100 kilometres (62 miles) away.

Why is the Ford name so famous?

Cars are everywhere today, but few of us know who actually invented them. Most of us do know the name of American inventor Henry Ford, however, because he is the one who first made cars that ordinary people could afford.

Henry Ford had very little education but he had imagination and good mechanical ability. In 1892, he perfected a new type of engine running on gasoline. He made his first car in 1896. Seven years later he set up the Ford Motor Company in Michigan, and six years after that, he introduced the Model T automobile. With the success of the mass-production assembly lines, the price of the Model T was reduced to $290, making it possible for more people to afford to own a car. From 1909 to 1925, the Ford Motor Company sold 15 million Model T automobiles.

DID YOU KNOW . . . Henry Ford was a well-known racing car driver.

Index